EDGE BOOKS™

THE KIDS' GUIDE TO

MAGIC TRICKS

by Steve Charney

CAPSTONE PRESS
a capstone imprint

Edge Books are published by Capstone Press,
1710 Roe Crest Drive, North Mankato, Minnesota 56003.
www.capstonepub.com

Library of Congress Cataloging-in-Publication Data
Charney, Steve.
    The kids' guide to magic tricks / by Steve Charney.
    p. cm.—(Edge books. Kids' Guides.)
    Includes bibliographical references and index.
    Summary: "Step-by-step instructions show how to perform a variety
of illusions and entertaining magic tricks"—Provided by publisher.
    ISBN 978-1-4296-8452-1 (library binding)
    ISBN 978-1-62065-229-9 (ebook PDF)
    1.Magic tricks—Juvenile literature. I. Title.
GV1548.C445 2013
793.8—dc23   2011048903

Editorial Credits
Aaron Sautter, editor; Tracy Davies McCabe, designer; Svetlana Zhurkin,
    media researcher; Sarah Schuette, photo stylist; Marcy Morin, scheduler;
    Laura Manthe, production specialist

Photo Credits
All photos by Capstone Studio/Karon Dubke except:

Shutterstock: Darren Whitt, cover (bottom); Katrina Brown (red drapes), cover and
    throughout; Olena Pivnenko, cover (background); Stephen Coburn (hand with
    wand), cover and throughout; Suto Norbert Zsolt (background), back cover and
    throughout; Toria (background), back cover and throughout; unkreativ (white
    shelf), 6 and throughout

Printed in the United States of America in Stevens Point, Wisconsin.
032012   006678WZF12

Table of Contents

WELCOME TO THE CLUB!

From ancient times to today, magicians have amazed people with mind-bending tricks. Magicians are a playful bunch who love to entertain people with incredible **illusions**. And now it's your turn! Grab your magic wand, and get ready to learn some awesome tricks.

THE RULES OF MAGIC

✶ Never reveal your secrets! If you share the secret behind a trick, it will ruin the fun for you and your audience.

✶ Practice, practice, practice! If you don't practice, your timing will be off, and you'll likely expose the secret to a trick. Practice the trick in front of a mirror 10 times. When you think you've mastered it, practice it 10 more times. Keep practicing until the trick looks smooth and natural.

✶ Be entertaining! Boring magicians are painful to watch. Find ways to keep the audience entertained. Tell jokes and stories as you perform your tricks. Be charming and smile. The audience is more likely to enjoy the show if they enjoy watching you perform.

illusion—something that appears to be real but isn't

PROPS

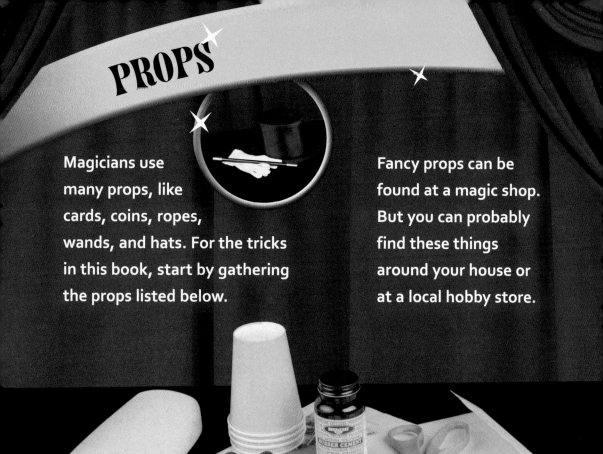

Magicians use many props, like cards, coins, ropes, wands, and hats. For the tricks in this book, start by gathering the props listed below.

Fancy props can be found at a magic shop. But you can probably find these things around your house or at a local hobby store.

baby powder
coins
deck of cards
dollar bill

envelope
handkerchief
newspaper
notepad
paper cups

pencil
plastic ring
rope
rubber cement
scissors

shoelaces
small craft
balls
thread

WHAT'S YOUR NUMBER?

What you need:
small notepad
pencil
envelope

For magicians, **predicting** the future is a piece of cake. A sealed envelope holds a number you can't possibly know. The audience won't believe it when you predict the exact number inside. It's easy once you know the secret.

Preparation:

❶ Write down three four-digit numbers on the first page of the notepad. Make the numbers look like three different people wrote them. Draw a line under the third number.

❷ Add up the numbers and write the total on a different piece of paper. Place the piece of paper in the envelope. Then seal the envelope and write "Prediction" on the front.

predict—to say what you think will happen in the future

6

Performance:

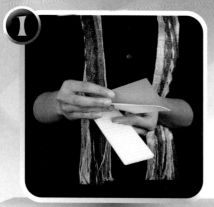

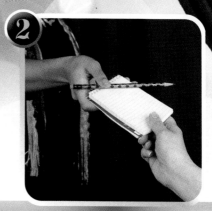

❶ Hand the envelope to someone in the audience. Say, "Please guard this with your life. Don't let anyone near it." Then open the notepad to the second page. Fold back the page with the prewritten numbers along with the cover. You don't want the audience to see this page.

❷ Pick someone in the audience and say, "Please write down a four-digit number." Then ask two more volunteers to write numbers below the first one. Ask the third person to draw a line under the numbers.

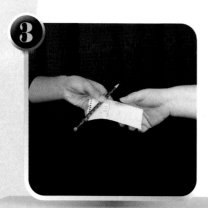

❸ Take back the pad and close it. Then ask the audience, "Who's good at adding?" When someone volunteers, rip out the secret page with the prewritten numbers. Ask the volunteer, "Would you add these numbers together, please?" Then ask him or her to say the number out loud.

❹ Finally, ask the person holding the prediction envelope to open it and read the predicted number out loud. The numbers match! Take a bow as the audience cheers your amazing mental powers!

RING AND ROPE

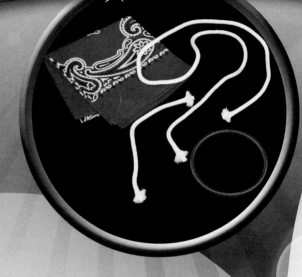

What you need:

piece of rope 3 feet (0.9 meter) long
piece of rope 8 inches
   (20 centimeters) long
5-inch (13-cm) plastic ring
large handkerchief or cloth

Preparation:

Don't throw this "life ring" and rope to a drowning magician. It's not much use when the rope comes loose in the blink of an eye. But don't worry—the magician just tricked you!

❶ Thread the short rope through the ring.

❷ Fold the long rope in half. Then hide the looped end in your hand along with the loose ends of the short rope. When you hold up the ropes, it will look like one long rope is looped through the ring. Hold the handkerchief with the other hand.

Performance:

❶ Start this trick by saying, "I once saw a magician drowning. I tried to throw him a life ring." Show the audience the ring dangling on the rope.

❷ Keep telling the story. "He grabbed the ring but went under the water. I couldn't see him!" Place the ring and rope on a table. Cover them and your hand with the handkerchief. Keep the loose ends of the long rope visible for the audience.

❸ Keeping your hand hidden under the handkerchief, remove the short piece of rope from the ring. Don't let the audience see how you do this step.

❹ Keep the short rope hidden inside the handkerchief. Grab both with your free hand and pull them away in one swift motion. Show the audience the separated long rope and ring. Then finish your story, "Suddenly the magician was standing next to me with the life ring and rope in his hand. It's magic!"

A HEARTY ASSISTANT

What you need:
deck of cards

Did you know that a playing card sometimes makes the best assistant? This special card won't just tell you where a chosen card is in the deck. It also has four aces up its sleeve!

Preparation:

❶ Place the five of hearts face up on the bottom of the deck.

❷ Place the four aces face down underneath the five of hearts on the bottom of the deck.

10

Performance:

❶ Ask a volunteer to pick a card. Tell the volunteer to look at it, but don't let you see it. Then have the volunteer place the card on top of the deck.

❷ Cut the deck of cards into two piles. Place the bottom half on top of the other half. The five and four aces will now be on top of the volunteer's card. Now say, "Have you met my assistant?" and fan out the cards to show that the five of hearts is the only face-up card. Say, "Here she is. Look, she's telling me your card is five more cards down."

❸ Count down five more cards from the five of hearts. This will be the volunteer's chosen card. Show it to the volunteer and audience and ask if it's the correct card.

❹ Finally, turn over the four aces. Say, "These guys are good helpers too. Meet David Blaine, David Copperfield, Harry Houdini—and some guy named Murray!"

POKING WASHINGTON'S EYE

What you need:
dollar bill
piece of paper 4 inches
    (10 cm) square
pencil

Preparation:

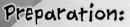

Ouch! Pushing a pencil through a dollar bill can be painful. Poor George Washington could get poked in the eye. But he can't tell a lie—it's just a trick!

❶ Fold the dollar bill in half with George Washington on the outside.

❷ Push down on the edge of the dollar at Washington's collar to create a secret pocket fold. The secret pocket should stop at the top of Washington's head. Press the creases tightly together. Then straighten the dollar so the secret folds aren't obvious.

Performance:

❶ Tell the audience, "Sticking a pencil through a dollar bill can be tricky. I don't want to poke George Washington's eye out!" Place the piece of paper over the dollar bill and fold them both in half. As you fold the dollar, recreate the secret pocket you made earlier. The piece of paper will hide it from the audience.

❷ Place the pencil between the dollar and the paper. Rest the pencil in the secret pocket.

❸ Push the pencil through the paper. Pretend that you heard someone shout as you do this. Say, "Oh no! Did you hear someone yell? I think I poked Washington's eye out."

❹ Pull the pencil out and straighten the dollar and paper. Show the audience that the paper has a hole in it. Finally, remove the paper and show that the dollar does not have a hole. Say, "It looks like George got lucky this time!"

THE MAGIC SHOELACE

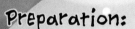

What you need:
long black pants
long piece of black thread
a small button
an extra shoelace that matches
the laces on your shoes

Preparation:

It can be easy to forget to tie your shoes before a magic show. If people point out your untied shoe, amaze them with this trick. Just shake your foot, and your shoe ties itself!

❶ Tie the thread around the center of the extra shoelace, and then run the shoelace down the inside of your pant leg. Let the ends of the shoelace dangle from both sides of your shoe. Make sure your pant leg hangs low enough to hide the shoe's real tied shoelace.

❷ Tie a button to the other end of the thread. Then place the button over the top of your pants where it won't be noticed and will be easy to grab later.

Performance:

1

2

❶ Be ready to do this trick when someone notices that your shoe is untied. If nobody does, show the audience the loose ends of the trick lace. Say, "I've gotten tired of tying my shoes the old-fashioned way. I found a much easier way to do it."

❷ Start shaking your leg and foot strongly. As you shake your foot, pull on the secret thread to pull the trick lace up your pant leg.

3

Tip: Be sure the trick shoelace is pulled up high enough before showing the audience the top of your shoe.

❸ Finally, pull up your pant leg to show the audience that your shoelace has magically tied itself!

15

HATFUL OF WATER

What you need:
two thin paper cups
a sturdy hat
a glass of water
scissors

Deep in the jungles of Africa is a special pool with magical powers. Water from the pool can move on its own! Tell this story before doing this trick, and your audience will be asking, "How did you do that?"

Preparation:

1 Carefully cut the bottom out of one cup and the rim off the second cup.

2 Place the bottomless cup inside the rimless one. Together, they will look like one whole cup.

16

❶ Place the hat and the trick cup on the table. Hold up the glass of water and say, "I got this magic water in the jungles of Africa. Its special powers will amaze you!" Then put the trick cup inside the hat.

❷ Hold the glass like you're going to pour the water into the hat. Say, "Wait a minute. That's not very magical!" Set down the glass of water. Reach into the hat and take out the bottomless cup. Be sure to leave the secret rimless cup inside the hat. Set the bottomless cup to the side, making sure the audience doesn't see that it has no bottom.

❸ Say, "To prove this water is magical, I'll pour it directly into the hat!" Pour the water into the hidden rimless cup. As you do this say, "Actually, this water doesn't like being poured out."

❹ Pick up the bottomless cup and slide it back into the rimless cup inside the hat. Say, "It really likes to be inside a container." Then pretend to watch the water move around inside the hat and into the trick cup.

❺ Take the trick cup out of the hat and pour the water back into the glass. Say, "Like I said, this magic water likes to be in a container." Then take a drink of the water and put the dry hat on your head. Take a bow as the audience applauds!

SHRINKING ADS

What you need:
a newspaper
rubber cement
baby powder

Preparation:

Extra! Extra! Read all about it! Shrinking newspaper remains unharmed! This trick is certain to keep the audience guessing. As a newspaper column is cut in two, it always stays in one piece!

❶ Cut out a column from the want ads of a newspaper. Lightly brush rubber cement on one side. After it dries, put on a second coat of rubber cement and let it dry.

❷ Lightly sprinkle baby powder over the sticky paper. Then brush off the excess powder.

Performance:

1 Hold up the newspaper column and show it to the audience. Say, "Mom always gave me the want ads to look for a regular job. But I told her that I wanted to be a magician!"

2 Fold the newspaper column in half with the secret sticky side inside. Use scissors to cut a piece off the paper a half inch down from the fold. Let the cut-off piece fall to the floor.

3 Slide your thumb and finger across the cut in a magical way. The rubber cement will keep the two pieces together. Now open the paper to show that it's still in one piece!

4 Repeat steps 4 and 5, but this time cut the paper at an angle. When you unfold it, the audience will be amazed when they see the paper is L-shaped. Say, "After I showed her this trick, Mom agreed that I'd make a great magician!"

Tip: You can repeat steps 2 and 3 several times before trying the angled cut.

CUPS AND BALLS

What you need:
three paper cups
five marble-sized soft
    craft balls

Just like ghosts pass through walls, these balls will pass right through cups. This ancient trick has a great finish. The balls pass through the cups again and again, and the last one goes right through the table!

Preparation:

❶ Place one ball in a cup.

❷ Place the other two cups inside the first one on top of the secret ball.

Performance:

❶ Place the stack of cups on the table. Place the other four balls in front of the cups. Say, "These powerful magic balls can pass right through a cup."

❷ Pick up the stack of cups and turn them over. The bottom cup holds the secret ball. Turn it over in a smooth motion onto the table to hide the secret ball under it. Then place the other cups to the right and left of the middle cup.

❸ Place one ball on top of the center cup.

❹ Now place the two side cups on top of the ball on the middle cup.

5 Say a magic word like, "Abracadooley!" and wave your hand over the cups. Pick up the three cups to show that the ball has magically dropped through onto the table.

6 Place the cups separately on the table again. The middle cup has a secret hidden ball. Place this cup over the ball on the table. There are now two balls hidden under the middle cup.

7 Place another ball on top of the middle cup. Then cover the ball with the two side cups as before.

8 Say another magic word like, "Abracapocus!" and wave your hand over the cups. Lift up the stack of cups to show that there are now two balls underneath. It looks like the second ball has magically dropped through the middle cup.

9 Now say, "These balls can go through two cups too!" Repeat the process as before, but this time place a ball on the second cup in the stack.

10 Say a third magic word like, "Hokus Jokus!" and wave your hand. Lift up the stack of cups to show that there are now three balls underneath.

11 Tell the audience, "These balls can even go through the table." Lift up the stack of cups. The top cup now has a hidden ball. Place this cup over the balls on the table, and put the other cups on the sides.

12 Take the final ball and hold it under the table. You can hide it in your lap. Knock on the underside of the table and say magic words like, "Abby Cadabby!" Finally, lift up the middle cup to show that there are four balls on the table!

Tip: It's best to use cups with lips on the bottom that can help hold the balls.

BEAM ME UP!

What you need:
four coins
four playing cards

In science fiction movies, it takes a lot of **technology** to transport people from a spaceship to a planet. But with this trick you can do it with a few coins and playing cards!

Preparation:

❶ Spread out four coins on a table in front of you. Hold the four cards in your hand.

technology—the use of science to do practical things

Performance:

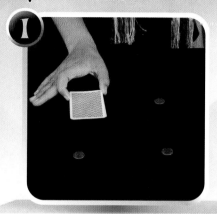

1 Place the four cards on top of one of the back coins. Say, "Have you ever seen movies where the crew transports from a planet to its spaceship? These coins can do it too!"

2 Pick up the cards again with both hands. As you do this, secretly grab the coin underneath them. Use a smooth motion so the audience can't tell you are picking up the coin.

3 Tip the cards down and slide the top card off to place it like you're covering the first coin again. It's important to use the cards to hide the fact that the coin is really missing.

4 Place two cards on top of the two front coins. The last card is secretly hiding the first coin you picked up. Place this card and the hidden coin over the last coin in back.

Tip: Be careful when putting coins down to avoid making any "clink" sounds. It could give away the fact that you are placing the hidden coins.

5 One back card has no coin under it, and the other back card has two coins under it. Now turn one of the front cards sideways and pick it up. As you do this, secretly grab the coin under it with your thumb. The coin will appear to have disappeared!

6 Say, "As you can see, these coins can transport through the air." With your other hand, lift up the back card that is hiding two coins under it.

7 Place the empty card to the side. Then place the card hiding the third coin on top of the two coins. There are now three coins under that card.

8 Say, "You really need to watch these coins closely." Repeat step 6 with the other front card. Now it looks like that coin has disappeared!

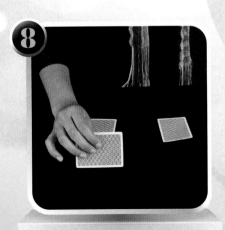

9 Tell the audience, "You never know when these coins are going to jump through the air." Lift up the last card to show that there are now three coins under it.

10 Place the empty card to the side. Then place the card that is hiding the last coin on top of the others. There are now four coins hidden under the card.

11 Pick up the first back card to show that the coin is missing.

12 Say, "Maybe someday we'll all be able to transport ourselves just like these coins." Lift up the last card to show the audience that all four coins are underneath!

Tip: Try adding some magical entertainment by snapping your fingers or waving your hand over the last card before revealing the hidden coins.

SQUIRMY WORMY

What you need:
3-foot (0.9-m) piece of rope
8-inch (20-cm) piece of rope

Preparation:

❶ Loop the short rope around the middle of the long rope.

Can a worm that's been cut in half be magically restored? It can with a little magic dust. Amaze your family and friends with this classic restored rope trick!

Performance:

❶ Hide the looped part of the ropes in your hand with the short rope ends pointing up and the long rope ends hanging down. From the front it looks like you are holding two long ropes. Say, "It's thought that if you cut a worm in half, it'll grow into two worms. I cut this guy in half earlier. But with a little magic, I can make him a single worm again."

❷ Tie the short rope into a loose knot around the long one. Use your hands to hide how the ropes are already looped together. Hold the knotted rope up and show it to the audience. Say, "It looks like this worm hasn't quite healed yet."

❸ Hold one end of the rope in your fist, and then start wrapping it around your hand. As you wrap it, secretly **palm** the knot in your other hand. Keep it hidden as you slide it off the rope. Now say, "I think I need some of my invisible magic dust!"

❹ With the knot hidden in your hand, reach into your pocket and pretend to grab some magic dust. Leave the knot in your pocket. Then pretend to sprinkle invisible magic dust over the rope that is wrapped around your hand. You can say some magic words as you do this.

❺ Slowly unwrap the rope and show the audience that the two pieces have magically become a single rope. Say, "I knew that magic dust would help put this guy back together." Then take a bow as the audience applauds!

palm—to secretly hide something in the palm of your hand

GLOSSARY

audience (AW-dee-uhnss)—people who watch or listen to a play, movie, or show

illusion (i-LOO-zhuhn)—something that appears to be real but isn't

palm (PALM)—to secretly hide something in the palm of your hand

predict (pri-DIKT)—to say what you think will happen in the future

technology (tek-NOL-uh-jee)—the use of science to do practical things

READ MORE

Barnhart, Norm. *Amazing Magic Tricks.*
Mankato, Minn.: Capstone Press, 2009.

Einhorn, Nicholas. *Stand-up Magic and Optical Illusions.* Inside Magic. New York: Rosen Central, 2011.

Lane, Mike. *Performing Magic.* Miraculous Magic Tricks. New York: Windmill Books, 2012.

INTERNET SITES

FactHound offers a safe, fun way to find Internet sites related to this book. All of the sites on FactHound have been researched by our staff.

Here's all you do:

Visit *www.facthound.com*

Type in this code: 9781429684521

 Check out projects, games and lots more at
www.capstonekids.com

Index